YEAH MON!

COME CHAT WID MI!

YEAH MON!
COME CHAT WID MI!

BY

CARMEN EARLINGTON

www.bookstandpublishing.com

Published by
Bookstand Publishing
Morgan Hill, CA 95037
4460_4

Copyright © 2016 by Carmen Earlington
All rights reserved. No part of this publication may be reproduced or transmitted in any form or by any means, electronic or mechanical, including photocopy, recording, or any information storage and retrieval system, without permission in writing from the copyright owner.

ISBN 978-1-63498-410-2

Printed in the United States of America

In loving memory of my mother, Pearl.

ACKNOWLEDGEMENTS

Thank you, Bevin, for your unwavering optimism and encouragement.

Thank you, Cruize, for your help and perseverance in bringing this idea to fruition.

I could not have done it without either of you.

Thank you to my many friends who helped me with the first project, much of which I have incorporated into this one.

CONTENTS

Acknowledgements vii
Introduction xi
PART I: COME CHAT WID MI 1
   Conjugation of Verbs 3
   Use of Pronouns 7
   Forming Plurals 9
   Pronunciation and Consonant Blends 11
   Negating Sentences 13
   Word Meanings 17
   Jamaican Proverbs 23
PART II: WORDS OF WISDOM FOR ALL OCCASIONS ... 65
PART III: TIME FI LAUGH 131
Glossary 141

x

INTRODUCTION

A Creole language is developed from the mixing or intertwining of parent languages. Jamaican patois (patwa), as the dialect is called, fits this category because the vocabulary consists mainly of English words, or a form of these words, combined with the grammar of the dialects spoken by the African slaves who were brought to the island in the seventeenth century, English being the dominant language, and the African dialects the subordinate group. Although a few words have survived from the African dialects of the slaves, most of the words used in the dialect today are of English origin.

Walk down the street of any foreign territory and mention that you are Jamaican, and almost immediately someone will issue the retort, "Yeah mon." Why these words have become the hallmark of being Jamaican I will never know; but if you are a fan of Jamaican music and other things Jamaican, then you might want to start learning the dialect/language. In the next few pages you will discover the basic structure and form of the language. Then you can test what you have learned by reading some jokes and proverbs that are unique to Jamaica.

Discover the wit and wisdom embodied in the Jamaican tradition and learn to laugh at yourself, because this is what Jamaicans do best. So come on and "Come chat wid mi."

PART I

COME CHAT WID MI

Carmen Earlington

CONJUGATION OF VERBS

Although the dialect used to be referred to as 'broken English' it is important to understand that it has a grammar and form that are different from those of English. A look at how verbs are conjugated in the dialect should prove very valuable.

Let's take a look at how the English verb "to come" is conjugated, and compare it with the conjugation of the same verb in the dialect.

I am coming
You are coming
He/She/It is coming
We are coming
You (pl.) **are** coming
They are coming

In the dialect this conjugation would be as follows:

Mi a come

Yuh a come

'Im/She a come

Wi (we) a come

Unoo (you pl.) **a** come

Dem (them) **a** come

Two things are worthy of note here. The verb endings in the dialect are not inflected. In the English conjugation the helping verb changes based on the subject (am, are, is). In the dialect it remains the same 'a'. As the speaker moves more toward Standard English, the form of the verb will change.

The "a come" form of the verb will likely change to 'comin' and this remains the same regardless of the subject. So the conjugation would now become:

Mi comin'

Yuh comin'

'Im/She comin'
'Wi comin'
'Unoo comin'
'Dem comin'

Tense is shown by adding a word in front of the verb instead of changing the verb in any way. For example, came, the past tense of come, in the dialect becomes did come. So **I came** becomes **mi did come**. **I ran** becomes **mi did run**. Context is also used to define tense. Often, a word that indicates time is placed before or after the verb.

Im come yesside/yestoday.

He came yesterday.

Then there is the mighty little word "**a**". In the dialect this word is hardly ever used as the indefinite article as it is in English. It has several other meanings. Depending on how it is used in a sentence, it may mean I, it, it is, am, are, or to.

(A) my book or a fi mi book.

(It is) my book.

(A mi) put it deh /A mi put it dere.

(It's me that) put it there or I put it there.

Mi **a** come.

I **am** coming.

Weh yuh **a** go?

Where **are** you going?

Mi goin' **a** school.

I am going **to** school.

USE OF PRONOUNS

Subject pronouns are seldom used in the dialect. Object pronouns (mi, 'im, dem – me, him, them) are also used as subject pronouns. 'Me' pronounced 'mi', is used as subject, object, and possessive pronoun. So are wi, (we), dem (them) and 'im (him).

Mi not goin'.
I am not going.

A fi **mi** book.
It is **my** book.

Give it to **mi.**
Give it to **me**.

The possessive pronouns — his, hers, ours, your(s), theirs — do not exist in the dialect. Neither does the apostrophe 's'.

His becomes 'fi him'.

These are his books. **A fi him book dem.**

Hers 'fi har'

This is her dress. **Dis a fi har dress.**

Ours 'fi wi'

Those are not our books.

Dem book deh a no fi wi.

Your(s) 'fi yuh'

Is this your car/Is this car yours?

A fi yuh car dis?

Theirs 'fi dem'

That house is theirs/That is their house.

A fi dem house dat.

The boy's shirt simply translates '**de bwoy shirt**'.

FORMING PLURALS

As was stated earlier, there is no inflection of word endings in the dialect. This is also true when pluralizing words. Plurals are indicated by either adding a number in front of the word to be pluralized or adding a qualifying word after the word to be pluralized. Hence:

About ten dawg rush mi.

About ten dogs rushed after (chased) me.

Mek mi si yu han dem.

Mek mi si yuh two han'.

Let me see both your hands.

In the first example, the number ten was used to indicate that there was more than one dog. In the second example the word 'dem' made it clear that the speaker meant not just one hand.

Carmen Earlington

PRONUNCIATION AND CONSONANT BLENDS

Very few languages produce the "th" sound as the English language does, and the Jamaican dialect is no exception. 'Th' in the dialect is often pronounced like 'd'; so these become dese, them is pronounced dem, and so on.

When these letters appear in front of a consonant, they are usually pronounced like 'ch'.

Words such as throw, through and three, become chrow, chrew and chree.

Sometimes the 'h' sound is omitted altogether and the 'th' blend is pronounced like a 't', as in the word think, which becomes 't'ink'. For example:

Mi did t'ink a mine.

I thought it was mine.

'Ture' is usually pronounced like 'cha'. Nature becomes nacha and picture becomes pickcha.

Double 't' in the middle of a word is usually pronounced like a 'c' or a 'k'.

Hence, bottle becomes **bockle**; little, **lickle**.

Words ending in 'er' are pronounced like they end in 'a'.

Mother, therefore, sounds like **modda**, and father like **fahda**.

NEGATING SENTENCES

NOH AND NAW

Both of these words mean not, but sometimes in slightly different contexts. Naw implies negation of a continuous action, and often implies defiance.

For example: Im naw eat.

He is not eating. He is not going to eat.

Im noh eat.

He does not eat or he did not eat.

Dem noh come.

They did not come. This may also be translated: They are not here.

Dem naw come.

They are not coming. They are not going to come.

Mi noh dweet.
I did not do it.

Mi naw dweet.
I am not going to do it.

Another feature of the Jamaican dialect is the order of words in questions or statements. Tense and word order are not very important. The same words said in the same order may be a command, a simple statement, or a question, depending on the inflection of the voice.

A fi me. (It's for me.) It is mine.
A fi mi? (Is it for me?) Is it mine?
Go now. Go at once. (imperative)
Go now? Should I go now?

In asking questions, the object pronoun is often left out.

Is mine? Is it mine? (the pronoun 'it' is omitted).

Yuh comin'? Are you coming?

The use of repetition for emphasis is another hallmark of the Jamaican dialect. For example, "mi laugh, mi laugh, mi laugh" so till, simply means, "I laughed a lot".

'Im fool, 'im fool, 'im fool' is emphasizing that he is really stupid.

Carmen Earlington

WORD MEANINGS

Many English words are used to convey different meanings in the dialect. '**Heap**' is one of those words. When this word is used in English, it means a pile of something. In the Jamaican dialect it means 'a whole lot of' or many. It is not uncommon to hear someone say 'a whole heap a people was dere,' meaning there was a great number of people there.

'**Again**' is another word that often carries a different meaning. In English it means another time, or that an action is repeated; but in the Jamaican dialect it can mean, 'Do you still intend to do something?'

English: Are you going to the store again? (meaning, are you making another trip to the store?)

Dialect: Yuh a go again?

This may convey the English meaning of the word 'again'; or it may be asking: Are you still going?

Ignorant in the dialect means 'hot-tempered.' To be described as dark (dawk) and ignorant is to be impolite and uncouth.

The word **'salt,'** when used to describe someone, denotes that the person is unlucky; and, in addition to being unlucky, is likely to extend their bad luck to anything or anyone they touch. Therefore, no one wants to be around a **'salt'** person.

Tea is also a very interesting word. It is used to refer to any hot beverage. Therefore, don't be surprised if someone asks you for a cup of chocolate tea, cocoa tea, coffee tea, or mint tea.

Be careful if asked for a **'couple'** of anything. Should you give just two of whatever you're asked for, as the English meaning of the word implies, you might be told how 'mean' you are. When someone asks for a couple of things, they usually mean that they would like a few of them; they certainly don't expect just two. To give just two would give the impression that you are **'mean'** (stingy).

If someone tells you to 'Do something and you will see,' that is not an invitation for you to do whatever they said you should do; neither will you see anything. For example, should you be told "**touch me an' yuh wi si**" (touch me and you will see), it simply means 'I dare you to touch me.'

The word "hush" carries an additional meaning in the dialect. If someone accidentally steps on your toes or bumps into you and says 'hush,' they don't mean that you should be quiet about it. They mean, 'I am sorry; please excuse me.'

Jamaica may be the only place where you will see a **'bull cow.'** Whereas in English the word cow refers to the mature female of cattle, in the Jamaican dialect it refers to both the male and the female of our domestic bovine animals. So, in order to differentiate between male and female, we describe them as "**modda** (mother) **cow**" and "**bull cow.**" The English word heifer (heifa) retains its meaning in the dialect. It is used to describe a young cow that has not yet had a calf.

The dialect also has its fair share of onomatopoeic words. There is no need to study them, because the sounds of these words are so aptly descriptive that you will be in no doubt as to what they mean. However, here are a few of them:

A **boogooyagah** person is someone who is untidy and uncouth. If your room is **chaka-chaka**, it is a real mess. And watch out if someone tells you that there will be **bangerangs** between you and them; this means that things won't be pleasant.

Tallawah is one word that says a mouthful. This word is often used to describe the Jamaican people in general. You may hear the phrase, "**Wi likkle but we tallawah.**" This phrase means, we may be small (a small country) but we are a force to be reckoned with.

So now that we have uncovered a few basics of the language, come practice your skills in the next section.

Carmen Earlington

JAMAICAN PROVERBS

One outstanding feature of the Jamaican dialect is that it is very precise and concise, and uses a lot of imagery. It allows one to speak a whole volume using only a few words.

Our unique proverbs, expressed in the dialect, originated from the images and everyday experiences of an agrarian society in which the way of life was simple. Thus, the messages they conveyed were easily understood by the hearer. Over the years, these words of wisdom have been used by our elders to teach, admonish, encourage, and instill in us the wisdom and moral values necessary for our life's journey.

So walk with me as we explore the wit, wisdom, and humor of the Jamaican people, expressed through our Jamaican proverbs.

"Mawga cow a bull mumma."

Translated, this proverb literally says that:

The meager and emaciated cow is the mother of a big bull or has the potential to become the mother of a big bull.

What did our grandparents mean when they quoted this proverb to us? They were telling us not to underestimate people, not to judge them by the way they look – especially in their later years. These people may have made valuable contributions to society. The way they look now may be the result of what they had to undergo to make their contribution to the community. Also, you never know the potential of those you tend to underestimate. Regardless of the way they look, they could have the ability to produce great things.

YEAH MON!

Mawga cow a bull mumma.

"One bellyful cyaan' fatten mawga cow."

One full stomach will not fatten the meager cow.

The cow did not become meager overnight, so one good meal will not improve its lot. It needs continuous nourishment over a period of time. I doubt very much that this proverb had anything to do with cows, but it is a very simple and graphic way to show that periods of extreme hardship are not overcome in a moment.

"Bad pastcha mek good sheep shabby."

A bad pasture will make good sheep look shabby.

People are affected by their environment. Often we cannot see a person's true worth or potential when circumstances of life have them in a bad situation. In other words, a bad environment may give a false impression of a person's true worth.

"Rock stone a river bottom noh know weh di one dem pon top a feel."

"Rock stone a river bottom noh know sun hot."

I have heard this saying quoted in both of the above ways. Both convey the same meaning:

The rocks at the bottom of the river have no idea what those outside of the water are feeling.

Of course not, because those at the bottom of the stream have the water constantly lapping over them, so that they do not feel the harsh rays of the sun beating down on them. Those that are out of the water, however, have to deal with the brutal heat of the sun's rays on a daily basis.

What do we learn from this? Where we are positioned in life affords us different perspectives. We should not judge another person based on our life experiences, especially those of us who lead comfortable lives, because unless we have been placed in a particular situation, we cannot understand the problems associated with it. Some of us have been placed in more fortunate positions than others, so even though we may share similar attributes, we should not judge another person from our vantage point.

"Sheep a sweat, but wool cova it."

The sheep is sweating, but no one can tell because of the wool over its skin.

You cannot tell about a person's life or circumstances by simply looking at their outward appearance. Therefore, do not compare yourself with others or envy their lives, because what you see may not be the whole story. Someone's life may seem enviable, when in fact it is not.

This advice was usually given when we tended to compare our circumstances with that of another person, believing that their life was better than ours.

"De way puss mew a noh soh 'im mouse."

The way the cat purrs (says "meow") is very different from the way in which the cat goes about catching mice.

Therefore, you cannot judge the cat's ability to catch mice based on the sound it makes when it is purring. The way it purrs may mislead you into believing that it is a gentle, harmless pet, when in fact it could be quite aggressive and adept at catching mice. I believe that this was our parents' very elaborate way of telling us not to judge people by their outward appearances.

"A noh every mango gat magitch."

Although it would not be surprising to find maggots in mangoes, not every mango has maggots.

Not everyone is the same. You have to judge each person on his own merit.

Things Are Not Always What They Seem to Be

"Pretty rose gat macka jook."

The beautiful rose has a prickly thorn.

No matter how beautiful or wonderful a situation, there is always a down side to it.

"Yuh shake man han', yuh noh shake 'im heart."

You shake a man's hand, you don't shake his heart.

A handshake may lead you to think that the person whose hand you shake is in agreement with you or shares the same sentiments, but you cannot know what he is thinking in his heart. It may be the opposite of what is denoted by the handshake. Don't read too much into outward gestures. You cannot read a person's mind.

"Noh care how boar hog try fe hide unda sheep wool, 'im grunt always betray 'im."

No matter how the boar hog tries to conceal itself in sheep's wool, his grunt will always betray him.

A boar hog can pretend to be a sheep all it wants, but the grunt coming from its mouth will tell everyone what he really is. As it is with the hog, so it is with people. We may pretend for a long time, but eventually our true character will come to light, and it is usually the things that come out of our mouths that betray us.

"Not every kin teet is a laugh."

Not every smile is genuine.

Sometimes a show of teeth is all that it is. The show of teeth may be hiding the true feelings.

"Tek kin teet cova hart bun."

Use a smile to cover your heartache.

This advice was not given to encourage us to be phony or hypocritical. Rather, it was saying, don't give in to your problems.

"Not everyting weh have sugar sweet."

Not everything that contains sugar is sweet.

Literally, there are many foods that contain sugar but are not sweet to the taste. The taste of the sugar is masked by the other stronger and less appetizing flavors. In life many things may appear enviable, but are not. The struggles involved in achieving them, or in keeping them once you have achieved them, rob them of their appeal.

FOCUS ON YOUR GOALS

"Nuh watch de noise a de market, watch de sale."

Don't watch the noise of the market, watch the sales.

Don't pay too much attention to the noise in the marketplace; don't be fooled by it. Look at how much is being sold. A noisy marketplace conveys the impression that there is a lot of business going on. That is not necessarily true. Sometimes the noise only covers the fact that there is nothing much going on.

The lesson: Keep your eyes focused on your goals, ambitions, or dreams. Don't be distracted by what others are saying about how well they are doing. They may just be making a lot of "noise." See if the results they are boasting about can actually be substantiated.

"Yuh lick i' lick i' till yuh bite i'."

You lick it and lick it until you are able to bite it.

This is another proverb about problem solving and taking small steps towards your goal. You may have something to eat that you are not able to bite into immediately, either because it is too hard or too big for you to get your mouth over it; but if you keep licking it for a while, you will eventually reduce it to a point where you can manage to bite it. In the same way, if you keep chipping away at a problem that seems insurmountable at the outset, little by little you will find that it becomes less intimidating and you are able to solve it.

There is also another way to interpret this proverb. Sometimes you are forced to put up with certain situations because you have no choice. So you 'kiss and cajole' until you gain the upper hand and are able to 'bite it' (express your true feelings).

"Every mickle mek a muckle."

While I never figured out what a mickle or a muckle was, the meaning was quite clear when this proverb was quoted to me. It bears a lot of resemblance to the previous one in that it is saying, every little bit counts.

"Yuh come fi drink milk, noh count cow."

You came to drink milk; do not count cows.

If your mission is to drink milk, then concentrate on drinking all the milk you can. You don't have to know how many cows there are. That is none of your business. In other words, don't lose sight of your purpose and start interfering in things that don't concern you.

"One one coco full basket."

If you pick up just one coco at a time and put it in your basket, eventually your basket will be full.

Why the coco? Well, for those who don't know what the coco is, it is a very small tuber, and it takes many of them to fill a basket. The lesson is this: If you take tiny steps towards your goal, whatever that goal may be, you will eventually realize it.

Carmen Earlington

One one coco full basket.

KNOW YOURSELF

"Noh heng yuh hat higher dan yuh han' cyan reach it."

Do not hang your hat higher than your hand can reach it.

In other words, do not hang your hat so high that you have to climb up to take it down. I remember asking my grandmother why I shouldn't do that. I was, of course, taking the words literally. She told me that in climbing up to take it down, I might fall and hurt myself. Those of us who have 'fallen and hurt' ourselves because of aspiring to live beyond our means can attest to the wisdom of this saying.

"Noh put yuself ina gallon pan wen noggin can hole yuh."

Don't attempt to measure yourself in a gallon container when you can fit yourself into a noggin.

To properly see the comparison in this proverb, a short lesson in measurements is necessary. We know that a gallon holds four quarts, and a quart holds two pints. A pint holds two half-pints and one half-pint holds two noggins. It therefore takes thirty-two noggins to fill a gallon container. Now, can you see the breadth of the comparison?

The lessons to be learned are: Know your limitations; don't be too pompous; don't overreach yourself; don't think of yourself more highly than you ought to; and be realistic.

To think that you need to measure something in a gallon measure that might not even fill up a noggin is to be out of touch with reality.

"Alligator shouldn' call hog long mout."

The alligator should not refer to the pig as having a long mouth.

The reason is obvious: The alligator has a much longer mouth. We need to be careful about criticizing other people's weaknesses when we suffer from those weaknesses ourselves.

"Big finga neva seh look ya."

The thumb (big finga) never says 'look here.'

The thumb never points towards itself. You can demonstrate this very easily. Hold out your hands, palm upwards; then make a fist. You will notice that while all the fingers are pointing towards the body, the thumbs are pointing in another direction. Like the thumb, we never see our own faults although we are quick to see the faults of others. Very often, the faults we are quick to point out in others are those we exhibit ourselves.

"Senseh fowl seh him a go a barber; guinea chick sey him a go to."

The asenseh fowl says he is going to the barber; the guinea chick says he is going too.

The problem is that the asenseh fowl (chicken) has a patch of feathers on top of its head. The guinea chick is quite bald. The lesson is, don't be a copy-cat. Your needs are very different from another person's.

"Monkey mus' know weh 'im gwine put 'im tail before 'im orda trousiz."

A monkey must know where it is going to put its tail before it orders trousers.

YEAH MON!

To the monkey, trousers may appear to be extremely fashionable, and it may believe that it has so much in common with man that it can go ahead and imitate him by wearing trousers. However, the monkey has a serious limitation in wearing this garment – the matter of its tail. What can we learn from this? Be knowledgeable about your particular situation before you follow the crowd. You may have particular limitations that preclude you from being a part of the popular trend.

Carmen Earlington

Monkey mus' know weh 'im gwine put 'im tail before 'im orda trouziz.

"Pat a cuss kettle seh him bottom black."

The pot is cursing the kettle about its black bottom.

This saying is particularly funny when you consider that at the time these proverbs were in popular use, most of the pots were made of iron; and not only was a pot's bottom black, but the entire pot was black.

So the kettle was probably less black than the pot. At any rate, they were all in the same boat, but the pot couldn't see that. Need I say more?

"Puss an' dawg nuh have same luck."

Cats and dogs don't have the same kind of luck.

Everyone is different. What works for one person might not work for another.

Carmen Earlington

Puss an' dawg nuh have same luck.

WARNINGS ABOUT GREED

"Licky-licky fly follow coffin go a hole."

Licky-licky is another unique Jamaican term which bears some explanation. Folks who are considered to be licky-licky are likely to be greedy; but more than that, they are people who are particularly happy to receive things that cost them nothing. They don't even care if the 'freebie' was gained by ill-gotten means.

Therefore, the licky-licky fly will follow the coffin (with the dead body inside, of course) to the grave, ecstatic about the feast it will be having, and not stopping to think that once it gets into the grave (hole) with the dead body, it will meet its demise as well.

The lesson to be learned is, 'freebies' come with a price tag. Do not be so consumed with greed that you cannot stop to count the cost. What appears to be free may actually cost you more than you think.

"Craben cow always tink de nex nayba ghinny grass fatta."

A greedy cow always believes that the next door neighbor's guinea grass is better.

Before we get into the meaning of this proverb, I think a word about guinea grass is necessary. This long-bladed grass was a wonderful multi-purpose commodity. A handful of guinea grass rubbed together in the hands outdid all the modern scouring pads and sponges in washing dishes, pots, and pans. Not only did it scour them well, but it had a beautiful fragrance. It was also a favorite treat for all animals that ate grass. (No wonder that the greedy cow was eyeing the neighbor's guinea grass.) Farmers, and others who owned cows and horses, could be seen in the evenings cutting bundles of this grass to take home to their animals.

Now, back to the moral of this saying: Folks never appreciate what they have. They always believe that what others have is superior to what they have, no matter how alike the commodities are.

"Greedy dawg lose him bone."

A greedy dog loses its bone.

This, I believe, is a direct reference to the story of the dog that was crossing a river and dropped its bone in order to grab the bone from the dog it saw in the water, which was, of course its own reflection. The lesson: Be content with what you have; don't be too greedy.

ADVERSITY

"Trouble ketch yu, pickney shut fit yu."

When trouble catches you (when you fall into trouble), you will find that you can fit yourself into a child's shirt.

This is another saying about doing the seemingly impossible when you find yourself in a bad situation.

"One tree fall dung, bud naw sleep a grung."

If one tree falls down, that will not cause a bird to sleep on the ground.

Birds usually live in trees; if the tree in which a bird lives falls down or is cut down, there is absolutely no reason for the bird to sleep on the ground. There are many other trees around. All it needs to do is find another tree and build its nest again.

What can we learn from this saying? If one source dries up, no need to feel sorry for ourselves and give up. Find another source and start over again.

"Chigga ketch goat, 'im fin' im masta house bottom."

When the goat gets chiggers, it quickly runs home and finds refuge underneath its master's house.

A chigger was the larva of a parasitic mite that irritated the skin and made it sore and swollen. Goats' feet were particularly susceptible to this mite, so when the goat was out and about and got chiggers it knew that it needed to get home to its master if it was to be helped. I would daresay that most houses in the rural areas were made so that the animals could go underneath the houses. This was their sanctuary particularly when it rained.

Like the goat, whenever we get into trouble we remember the comforts of home.

"Rain a fall, but dutty tough."

Rain is falling, but the ground remains hard.

Blessings are flowing, but the needs are so great that hardships remain.

"Hard time mek dawg chaw razor."

Tough times will make a dog chew on razor blades.

Anyone who has ever handled a razor knows how likely it is to be injured by just picking one up. Imagine a dog being so hungry that it will attempt to chew razor blades. The lesson here is that when faced with great hardship one will attempt to do what would normally be considered impossible; in other words, tough times will motivate you to attempt the impossible.

YEAH MON!

Hard time mek dawg chaw razor.

"When man got bad luck, wet paypa cut him."

When a man is down on his luck, even wet paper will cut him.

That is, it doesn't take much to increase his downward spiral. Even the most innocuous circumstance will aggravate his condition. This saying I find particularly dramatic. Everyone knows that wet paper is soft and practically worthless. Imagine the likelihood of wet paper cutting someone.

RELATIONSHIPS

"Dry peas no full basket a mawnin won' full it a evenin'."

If dried peas/beans do not fill the basket in the morning, they certainly won't fill it at the end of the day.

For those of you reading this who have no "agricultural" experience, here's a short lesson about drying peas. When peas and beans are harvested, they are very plump and moist. Whatever portion is not consumed immediately is dried in the sun to preserve its shelf life. As the sun dries the moisture out of the peas, they get smaller and less plump. So, if the peas did not fill the basket when they were plump and moist, they certainly won't fill it when they have been dried out and shrunken by the sun.

The lesson here is: If you didn't appreciate my worth when I was younger, or at the beginning of the relationship, you certainly won't appreciate me when I am older, or when the novelty has worn off the relationship.

"Same knife weh stick sheep wi stick goat."

The same knife that the butcher uses to kill (stick) a goat will be the same one he uses to kill a sheep.

The same treatment that was meted out to one person is likely to be meted out to you as well. This is another admonition about relationships, particularly when someone has left a spouse to seek a new relationship with another. The "new" spouse was usually given this warning.

"Ole fire stick easy fi ketch."

Old fire sticks ignite easily.

If you are accustomed to making fires, you will know that having some fire sticks that were charred from a previous fire is a sure way to get a new fire going. This saying was usually attributed to lovers who had separated and were looking to get back together again. It meant that it shouldn't take long for the 'fires' to start burning between them again.

MIND YOUR OWN BUSINESS

"Yuh no put clothes a doh, yuh no look fe rain."

Because tense is not an important feature in the Jamaican dialect, this idiom may be interpreted in two different ways.

One interpretation is: *If you don't hang your clothes outdoors, you won't need to be watching for rain.*

A second interpretation is: *Since you didn't hang your laundry outdoors, you shouldn't be watching for rain.*

The lesson from the first interpretation: It is only when we have a vested interest in something that we pay attention to it, because it affects our interest.

The lesson from the second interpretation: Mind your own business. Why watch for "rain" when you have no reason for doing so?

"Cockroach no business in a fowl fight."

Cockroaches have no business in a fight between fowls (chickens).

Cockroaches are prey to chickens. Therefore, no matter what the circumstances, a cockroach should never attempt to be a peacemaker in a fight between chickens because chickens will easily forget their animosity for one another for a moment in order to devour the cockroach.

The meaning of this saying is pretty self-explanatory: Do not intervene in situations that don't really concern you, especially when you are the outsider. Allow "chickens" to solve their own problems.

"No cup nuh bruk, no cawfe nuh trow weh."

No cups were broken; no coffee was spilled.

There is nothing to make a fuss about. Leave well alone.

OUR ACTIONS HAVE CONSEQUENCES

"Play wid fire yuh mus' get bun."

If you play with fire, you will get burned.

If you court dangerous situations, you will eventually reap the consequences; that is, you'll find yourself in real danger.

"A no di same day leaf drop a water it rotten."

The leaf does not rot on the same day that it falls into the water.

The consequences of our actions often do not affect us immediately, but they do catch up with us eventually. Do not think you have gotten away with something simply because you do not pay the penalty immediately.

"If yuh lie wid dawg, yuh mus ketch flea."

If you lie down with dogs, then you will get their fleas.

People usually take on the characteristics of the company they keep.

"Wen rat like fi romp roun' puss jaw, one day 'im gwine en' up in a puss craw."

The rat that likes to play around (near) the cat's jaw will one day end up in the cat's craw (stomach).

This is another proverb that speaks of the foolhardiness of cavorting around dangerous situations. If a rat is stupid enough to play near the mouth of its sworn enemy, the cat, then it will eventually become the cat's dinner.

"Willful wase mek woeful want."

Willful waste makes woeful want.

If you purposely waste things, you will live to regret it. This was one of my grandfather's favorites. He would tell it to us especially when we would feed our dinner to the dogs, particularly those slices of yellow yam which he worked so hard to produce and which we hated so much. Needless to say, his words have come true. How I remember his words when I now have to pay an enormous price for the same commodity that I treated with such disdain as a child.

"Ole woman a swear fi eat gumma, an' gumma a swear fi run ole woman belly."

The old lady is swearing (threatening) to eat the gumma bean, and the gumma bean is threatening to give the old lady diarrhea.

The old lady is determined to do what she plans to do, and of course she can only see things from her vantage point. The gumma, however, is making plans of its own — only the old lady knows nothing about it. How similar is this to real life? We are so intent on carrying out our purposes that we never stop to think that there may be repercussions.

"Every day yuh carry bucket go a well, one day de bucket battam gwine drop out."

Every day you take the bucket to the well; one day the bottom of the bucket is going to fall out.

Maybe if many wrongdoers had learned this proverb they would have ceased their wrongdoing before their actions caught up with them, because that is basically what this saying is all about. You may be engaging in wrongdoing for a long time and getting away with it, but one day your luck will run out.

DON'T BE UNGRATEFUL OR FOOLHARDY

"Yuh cyaan' tan pon cow back cuss cow."

You cannot stay on the cow's back and curse the cow.

Why? You are benefiting from the cow. Don't bad-mouth something from which you are reaping a benefit. Do not be ungrateful.

"De tree weh shelta yuh wen rain a fall, no cut it dung wen sun hot."

The tree that sheltered you when it was raining, don't cut it down when the sun is shining.

Whatever or whoever helped you out when you were in a bad situation, don't discard it or them as soon as things appear to be going well. Chances are that you may need that source again even though it does not appear so at the moment. The true meaning of this saying is, "Don't be ungrateful."

"Yuh noh done cross riva noh trow weh yuh stick."

If you have not completely crossed the river, don't throw away your walking stick (cane).

It may appear that you have crossed the most dangerous parts of the river and are no longer in need of the support of your "walking stick." But that may be very deceptive. Even when you are close to the river bank, you may still need that stick to help you across.

Don't assume that you have "arrived" until you are very certain that you have.

"Rata belly full, im seh pitata got skin."

When the rat's stomach is full, it says the potato has skin.

When the rat was hungry, it ate the potatoes until its stomach was full; but once its stomach became full, it suddenly noticed that there was peel (skin) on the potatoes that made them inedible. Apparently the peel became a problem only after the rat's stomach was full.

As it is with the rat, so it is with us humans. When we are in desperate need, we will use any means necessary to climb out of our bad situation. But once we believe that we have overcome our particular problem, we will begin to be disdainful of the very thing that helped us out.

Carmen Earlington

PART II

WORDS OF WISDOM FOR ALL OCCASIONS

Carmen Earlington

"Tidde fi mi, tomorrow fi yuh."

Literally, this translates to:

Today for me, tomorrow for you.

If I am experiencing difficulties today, don't gloat; tomorrow it might be your turn to experience trouble. This may be directly translated to the English proverb: "Every dog has its day."

"Wat gawn bad a mawnin' won' come good a evenin'."

What has gone bad in the morning won't improve (come good) in the evening.

If something started out badly, it will usually end the same way.

"Chicken merry, hawk deh near."

When the chicken is happy, the hawk is close by.

The chicken is prey to the hawk. Sometimes we become so happy and carefree that we forget the dangers lurking nearby, and so we are prone to be swallowed up by them.

"Unfair game play twice."

Games played unfairly usually have to be replayed.

Lesson: Be fair in all your dealings.

"Quatty buy trouble, poun' cyan' cure i."

In order to understand this saying, it is necessary to explain the meaning of "quatty" and "poun'". Jamaica used to be a British colony, and therefore used British currency — not the new British currency, which is based on the decimal system, but the old currency, which used pounds, shillings, and pence.

There were twelve pennies in one shilling, and twenty shillings in one pound. Thus, there were two-hundred and forty pennies in one pound. There was also the ha'penny (half-penny); and the farthing, which was a quarter of a penny. The Jamaican culture made further divisions to this currency. Quatty, for example, was one and a half pennies.

So, literally speaking, one-and-a-half pennies can buy you so much trouble that one pound (two-hundred and forty pennies) won't be able to cure it (rid you of it). In essence, don't court trouble. It is easy to fall into trouble, but extremely difficult to get out of it. A 'little' trouble can bring you a lot of grief.

"Duppy know who fe frighten a dark night."

A ghost knows who to scare on a dark night.

"Goat look in a yuh face before 'im put 'im nose in a yuh basket."

A goat looks in your face before deciding whether it should stick its nose in your basket.

These two proverbs carry a similar meaning. Literally, if a ghost knows who to "frighten" on a dark night, then this suggests that it does not scare everyone. It will scare only those it knows will be scared. Similarly, if a goat looks in your face before deciding whether or not it is safe to put its nose in your basket, then that means it wouldn't put its nose in everybody's basket; there is something that it sees on your countenance or in your expression which tells it that it is safe to do so.

Therefore, these sayings suggest that we are responsible in large part for the way others treat us, and that people disrespect us only with our permission. In other words, it is we who give others permission to take liberties with us.

"Mine cow foot pay fe fowl foot."

Be careful lest you have to use a cow's foot to repay the debt for a chicken's foot.

This was a favorite of my grandfather's. He used this a lot when he warned us against the dangers of borrowing. You may borrow something from someone that is worth very little, but if it falls apart while it is in your keeping you may have to replace it with a new or much better one. And the worst of the matter is that although you have in essence bought one, you still don't own one.

"Beg water cyaan' bwile cow foot."

You cannot beg (enough) water to boil a cow's foot.

Why? It requires a lot of water to boil a cow's foot. No one is going to give you that amount of water. You will need your own supply of water. In other words, be independent; have your own source.

(And, for those who may not be familiar with this culture, and are wondering why anyone would want to boil cow's feet, let me just say that "cow's foot" makes a very tasty dish. You should try it sometime.)

"If yuh no walk unda fowl roos' fowl cyan' filt pon yuh."

If you don't walk under the fowls' roost, then you are not likely to get droppings from the fowls on your head.

For the young people who have never seen a fowl roost, let me just say that it was a very messy place. There was usually one particular tree on which the fowls roosted (slept), and over a period of time both the tree and the area underneath it was a horrible mess.

Walking under a fowl roost suggests doing something beneath your dignity, compromising your standards. Fowls don't really fly over your head. In order for them to get their droppings on your head, you have to put yourself in their territory. You have to get beneath them. The lesson here is: Don't compromise your standards; and don't provide others with an opportunity to disrespect you, especially folk who would only be too happy to comply.

"De higher monkey climb, a de more 'im expose."

The higher the monkey climbs, the more he exposes himself.

From a very literal viewpoint, as the monkey climbs higher in the tree, the more its private parts become visible to those below. Likewise, as people climb the ladder of success, their private lives and their actions become more open to scrutiny.

I don't know why the monkey was the animal of choice in this proverb, except that it probably imitates human behavior more than any other animal.

"Too much rat never dig good hole."

Too many rats never dig a good hole.

Well, how is that? All rats are supposed to be expert at digging holes. The problem is, with everyone being an expert at how to do the same thing, no one is willing to take instruction or follow a leader. There is therefore no teamwork. Too much expertise in the same area will kill a project.

"Puss gone, rat tek charge."

When the cat (puss) is away, the rats take over.

Cats are often used to keep rats under control. Therefore, when the cat is away, the rats seize the opportunity to have a good time.

In the absence of the boss, everybody becomes boss, or gets lax on the job.

"Wen yuh han ina tiga mout, yuh haffe tek time draw it out."

When your hand is in a tiger's mouth, you have to pull it out gently.

When you are in a dilemma over which you have little or no control, you need to practice good sense, and try to extricate yourself in such a way that you will not aggravate the problem and make matters worse.

"Big blanket mek man sleep late."

Literally:

A large blanket will cause a man to oversleep.

Here, a large blanket is used to denote comfort. If a man has a small blanket, it would not cover him sufficiently for him to get too comfortable. (He might still be a little cold.) Therefore, he would not be likely to remain in bed when he should be up and about. The lesson here is that there is a downside to being too comfortable.

"One tief nuh like see noder tief wid long bag."

One thief does not like to see another thief carrying a long bag.

Folks do not like competition, especially when they are engaging in the same type of trade. They always believe that the competition is doing better than they are, and of course they hate that.

"Man a plan, God a wipe out."

While man is making his plans, God is erasing them.

We can make all the plans we want, but if God does not approve of them He does not allow them to come to fruition.

"Hard ears pickney bite rockstone."

"Hard ears sheep belong to butcher."

"Hard ears pickney bun a sun hot."

The term "hard ears" means stubborn, hardheaded, will not listen.

Hardheaded children (pickney) will bite rocks. Stubborn sheep belong to the butcher. Stubborn children will burn in the sun.

All these sayings are warnings to children who do not listen to parental advice. They are admonitions that a stubborn child will have a very difficult life and is likely to experience grief.

"Empty barrel mek de mos' noise."

Empty barrels make the most noise.

You can prove this for yourself. In case you have never heard the clatter of empty barrels being transported anywhere, just use a stick to strike an empty barrel. Then use the stick to strike a barrel that's filled with something. You will notice a vast difference in the volume of the sound that emanates from each barrel. As it is with empty barrels, so it is with empty-headed people. They are always chattering but managing to say nothing.

"Time longer dan rope."

Time is longer than rope.

One can get to the end of a rope, but no one can get to the end of time, so there is always enough time for our actions to catch up with us.

"Long road draw sweat, short cut draw blood."

The long route draws sweat (from your body); the shortcut may draw blood.

If you take the long route, it will most likely take you a long time to get to your destination; you will quite likely be sweaty and tired. The shortcut, on the other hand, will get you there more quickly, but is often a very dangerous route. You might even lose your life traveling that route. 'Shortcut' as used in this proverb may be interpreted as less than scrupulous means, while 'long road' denotes honesty and diligence.

The moral of this proverb is that, pursuing your goals in an honest and diligent manner will take a lot out of you, but it is certainly more preferable than using unscrupulous means. Taking the long route will only make you sweat, but short cuts are likely to be dangerous.

"Whey yuh noh know cyaan' hurt yuh."

What you don't know won't hurt you.

Although this is not particularly true in all contexts, I think what our elders meant was that if you don't hear what others are saying about you, you won't be affected by it.

"Hawse cyaan' too good fe carry him own grass."

A horse shouldn't feel too good to carry its own grass.

A horse should not think that it is beneath its dignity to carry the grass that it is going to eat. Similarly, folk should not shirk from doing something that is of benefit to them.

"Hat needle bun tread."

A hot needle burns the thread.

Hot needle refers to haste, impatience. Thus, haste and impatience will ruin things.

"Whe noh dead noh dash wey."

If something is not dead, don't throw it away.

Don't discard a thing until you are sure it is dead (useless).

"Man noh dead noh call 'im duppy."

Don't refer to a man as a ghost until you are sure he is dead.

These two proverbs have very similar meanings. What they are saying in essence is that while there is life, there is hope.

"Yuh cyaan' tek fowl fat fry cow skin."

You cannot use the fat from a fowl (chicken) to fry cow's skin.

Think about how much fat you can find in a chicken. Imagine using that amount of fat to cook something as large and as tough as cow's skin. Here is another example of how our elders used proportions and comparisons to teach a lesson.

Let's say someone offends you. You should not attribute this person's actions to his or her entire family or attempt to seek vengeance on the entire family. Keep things in perspective; don' blow them out of proportion.

"Yuh cyaan' tek pop gun kill alligator."

You cannot use a pop gun to kill an alligator.

I have come to understand that in the present Jamaican culture, a pop gun refers to something far different from what the children in my generation knew it to be, and to what this proverb refers. A pop gun was a child's toy. For those born in the technological age who have no idea what a pop gun looked like, or for those to whom it means something different, let me give you a brief description.

A pop gun was made from a section of a small bamboo reed, and required a smaller stick that could be inserted into this reed. The shots for this gun (in the area where I grew up) were usually apple blossoms inserted into each end of the larger reed. The smaller stick was used to push the 'shots' out of the larger reed. This created a popping sound — hence, the name pop gun.

While it has been known to sting the skin or injure the eye if fired at either one, the pop gun would be quite harmless in injuring an alligator. You need to use a real gun if you wish to kill an alligator. There are two underlying messages here. One is that you need the appropriate tools to perform a job. But more importantly, in the words of the old cliché, "You cannot give a boy a man's job to do."

"Man dead, tree grow up to him door mouth."

When a man is dead, trees may grow up to his front door.

The inference is that the man would never have allowed that to happen when he was alive; but of course, now that he is dead, he is not able to do anything about it. The message here is, when we are no longer able to take care of our own affairs, we have very little say in the way they are administered. Our wishes are overridden and we just have to accept it. I am sure that everyone who knew the dead man knows that he would never have allowed his property to end up looking the way it did; but, at the same time, no one feels obligated to keep it the way he did.

"Scawnful dawg lik dutty puddin'."

A scornful dog will lick dirty pudding.

The dog that scorns everything finds itself in a position where it is forced to eat dirty pudding. This was an admonition to refrain from being filled with pride, because situations and circumstances of life may force you to stoop to the very same conditions you once thought were beneath you. I guess this was our fore-parents' graphic way of telling us that a haughty spirit precedes a fall.

"Ashes cowl, dawg sleep in deh."

When ashes get cold, dogs sleep in them.

When we get older, people take liberties with us that they would never have dared to take when we were younger. But, of course, now that the "fire" has gone out, they seize their opportunity, because they believe they will get away with it.

"Wen kitchen dressa tumble dung, mawga dawg laff."

When the kitchen dresser falls over, the meager dog laughs.

In order to fully understand this proverb, a short lesson about that special contraption — the kitchen dresser — is necessary. This was a makeshift table attached to one wall of the kitchen and having two legs in front. These kitchens were usually not a part of the house, but a separate building next to the house. Oftentimes it was not particularly sturdy. In addition to holding the pots and pans, it also held the bowl with the pickled fish and corned meat. At times dinner was also left on the 'dresser' for those who were absent at mealtime.

No wonder the meager (deprived) dog was highly elated when the dresser fell over, because it knew it would have a feast. In the same way, people who are deprived are often elated at the misfortunes of others, especially when they can benefit from those misfortunes in some way.

"Wan finga cyaan' ketch lice."

You cannot use one finger to catch lice.

Another variation of this proverb is:

"One han cyaan clap."

You cannot clap with one hand.

From a literal standpoint, you need more than one finger to catch lice and both hands in order to clap.

Both of these proverbs are speaking about the value of cooperation.

"To much callaloo mek peppa-pot soup bitta."

Putting too much callaloo in pepper-pot soup will make it bitter.

Callaloo is a vital ingredient in pepper-pot soup, yet too much of it in the soup will make it bitter. Don't overdo a good thing.

"Han' go, paki come."

The hand goes out; the paki comes back.

When you give, you always get back, and more than you give.

A word about the paki. The paki is a gourd. This gourd used to be picked and cut in half, and the contents scraped out. Then it was washed clean and put to dry. The dried paki now had a new name, "calabash." The paki, or calabash, was then used as a bowl. Therefore, the proverb is saying: You give someone a handful, you get in return a paki full (much more than you gave).

"Cow neva know di use o' him tail till fly tek it."

A cow does not know the usefulness of its tail until its tail becomes infested by flies.

Then it finds out that a tail is useful for swishing the flies away. We do not appreciate what we have until adverse circumstances force us to do so.

"Hog seh di fuss wata 'im ketch, im wash."

The hog says it washes in the first water (or mud hole) it finds.

The lesson for us is: When an opportunity presents itself, grasp it quickly.

"Cuss-cuss no bore hole ina skin."

Cursing and bad-mouthing people will not bore holes in their skin. The things that people say about you cannot really impede your progress.

"Rabbit cyaan' weigh more dan 'im four qua'ta."

A rabbit cannot weigh more than its four quarters.

For that matter, neither can any other animal. I have never been able to figure out why the rabbit was chosen to illustrate this proverb, but what it is saying in essence is that a rabbit cannot weigh more than its weight. The take-home message here is that we should not expect from anyone more than they are capable of doing.

"If rain fall an' yuh noh ketch no water, noh go roun' shakin tree afterward."

If it rained and you did not catch any water, don't go out and shake the trees to find water after the rain has stopped.

To put this very simply, make use of opportunities when they come your way.

"Any ting weh unda jackass belly gwine one day come pon him back."

Whatever is (hiding) under the jackass' belly will one day climb onto its back.

One day all the secrets that you are hiding will come to light.

"Idle jackass folla cane trash go a poun'."

The idle donkey follows the cane trash to the animal pound.

There is no need to explain what will happen to the donkey when it gets to the pound, but it is important to take note of how he got there. The sugar cane is a favorite treat of the donkey, but there is no substance in the trash of the sugar cane. Yet he allowed himself to be lured to the pound by it.

Secondly, if he had had something to do, he might not have resorted to such behavior. So the donkey got itself impounded by following after something that is totally worthless. What does this mean for us? Don't lose your freedom or get into trouble over worthless stuff. Inactivity and laziness create many problems.

"Tie yuh toe before it cut."

Tie your toe before it gets cut (a wound).

Why the reference to tying your toe? Well, before "Band Aid" became a household name, wounds were usually cared for with a home dressing and wrapped with a clean strip of cloth, the ends of which were tied to keep it secure. Also, during those times, the toe was a common target for cuts and bruises because many people only wore shoes on special occasions.

Hence, the warning to tie your toe before it actually gets hurt means you need to be prepared. Don't wait until problems overtake you to start figuring out what to do. It is useful to anticipate problems sometimes.

"A noh every shower a rain fall fi wet yuh."

You do not have to get wet from every shower of rain that falls.

You do not need to be involved in everything.

"If shark come from sea come tell yuh seh alligator raw, yuh mus' believe him."

If a shark comes out of the sea and tells you that alligators have a raw smell, you should believe the shark.

Why should you believe the shark? Well, think about it. Do you have a better way of finding out the truth of the matter? Can you face the alligator to find out for yourself if it is raw? Both the shark and the alligator have much in common; the shark is in a better position to know how the alligator smells than you will ever be.

What is the lesson behind this proverb? You need to take the word of someone who is in a position to know more about a subject than you are. Sometimes, trying to find out about some things firsthand is not in your best interest.

"All hog eat coco, but a only some it choke."

All hogs like to eat the coco (yam) but only some of them choke on it.

We all engage in wrongdoing at some time or another, but only some of us get caught. Therefore, there is no need for those of us who escaped retribution to feel superior to those who got caught doing the same things that we did.

"Betta chicken go fine puppy dead, dan puppy go fine chicken dead."

It is better — at least for the puppy — *for the chicken to go and find that the puppy is dead, than for the puppy to discover the chicken dead.*

It is hardly likely that anyone would blame the chicken for the death of the puppy, but the puppy would have a hard time convincing anyone of its innocence in the death of the chicken, even though it might not be in any way responsible for the chicken's death. The fact that chickens have been known to die at the 'paws' of puppies certainly does not help the puppy's cause.

What can we learn from this? First, it is difficult to live down a bad reputation. Second, it is easy to be maligned simply for being who you are.

"Yuh cyan' lef mongoose fi watch chicken."

You cannot leave chickens in the care of a mongoose.

To do so would be to provide the mongoose with its favorite meal; the mongoose just loves to eat chickens. Because we are neither mongoose nor chickens, what were our parents trying to tell us? We should never tempt a person with his weakness.

"De gum olda dan de teet."

The gums are older than the teeth (were around before).

They are also the foundation for the teeth.

The 'gums' represent our elders. They've been around before us, and have more wisdom. They have gone from just gums to teeth to gums again. So, even though the gums may not be as attractive as the teeth, they have something that the teeth have not yet acquired — the wisdom that comes from experience. In other words, respect your elders.

"Head olda dan grey hair."

The head is older than the grey hairs on it.

This proverb is very similar in meaning to the previous one. Grey hairs are usually a sign of old age, but one has to remember that the head was around long before the gray hairs came.

"Blood ticker dan wata."

Blood is thicker than water.

The 'blood' here is used to denote the special bond between relatives. Even if they don't get along well, they will band together against an outsider. They will not tolerate an outsider taking 'liberties' with relatives.

"Han' a bowl, knife a troat."

There are those that will be sharing a meal with you, eating from the same bowl, and at the same time, ready to put a knife to your throat.

This is a proverb about the treacherous nature of some people.

You should be aware that there are many people who will appear to be friends with you, but who would not think twice about hurting you if it furthered their cause.

"Every hoe have 'im tick a bush."

Every hoe has a stick in the bush (suited especially for it.)

There is someone for everyone. Everyone has a perfect partner somewhere.

"Trouble noh set like rain."

Troubles do not "set" like rain (gather like rain clouds do before it rains).

Rain clouds gather before it rains and hide the sun, so one can anticipate rain. However, troubles don't give a warning before they strike. They usually happen unexpectedly.

"De same dawg weh carry bone go, carry back one."

The same dog that carries a bone away will carry one back.

This saying has to do with gossiping and tattle-tailing. The person who likes to tell you what others are saying about you is likely telling those same people what you are saying about them.

"Jancro waan go a low lan, likkle breeze carry him."

The John Crow wanted to go to lower ground. A very light breeze brought him there.

It is important to note that the light breeze only helped him along because he had already resolved to go. Without this resolve the breeze would have had no impact on him.

In the same way, we use any excuse to propel us along in our decisions once we've made up our minds about a course of action.

"Tan an' see nuh spwile no dance, but intaferance mash it up."

To stand and observe what is going on won't spoil the dance or the party; but to jump in and interfere, especially when you have no idea what you're doing, might spoil things.

What is the lesson here? It is useful to observe and see how things are done before taking part.

"Yuh neva see smoke widout fiya."

You never see smoke without a fire.

Smoke does not appear out of the blue. It is an indication that there is a fire close by; the fact that you can't see the fire doesn't mean that it is not there. In the same way, there is a root cause behind people's behaviors and actions.

"Carry-go, bring-come bring misery."

Gossiping and tattle-tailing create misery in people's lives.

"Finga stink, yuh cyaan' cut it off dash weh."

If your finger stinks, you can't cut it off and throw it away.

To do that would be to hurt your whole hand and your body as well. Moreover, we need all our fingers. It is far better to put up with the odor of the finger while you try to nurse it back to health.

That "stinking" finger represents some of our family members who we would just love to discard. They embarrass the family; they refuse to embrace family values. They are just generally 'black sheep.' However, this proverb is telling us that casting off those relatives does not really help the family unit. We need to embrace them, and do all we can to help them.

"Betta fi eat yuh own green food dan yuh neighba ripe one."

It is better to eat your own green food than your neighbor's ripe one.

In the Jamaican dialect, the word green, when used to describe food, does not necessarily refer to color. It often refers to something being unfit — not properly matured or ready for harvesting. Hence, what the proverb is saying is that it is better to eat your food that is not quite fit than to steal your neighbor's food that is more fit. This needs little explanation. The lesson is, be content with what you have.

"Bite yuh lip before yuh open yuh mout, an' tase yuh wud before yuh talk."

Bite your lip before you open your mouth to speak, and taste your words before you do speak.

This was an admonition to think carefully before you open your mouth to speak, and when you do open your mouth, to choose your words with care.

"A no fi want a tongue mek cow no talk."

Literal translation:

It's not for want of a tongue why the cow does not speak.

The tongue is a vital organ in the production of speech; no speech can be produced without it. Yet the cow has a large tongue, but does not speak. If having a tongue gave you the right to speak, then the cow would certainly have a lot to say. The lesson for us is: Don't go chattering away simply because you have a tongue and are able to speak.

As I have grown older, though, I think I see a more profound wisdom in this saying. Not only does the cow not speak, but it cannot speak even though it possesses a most important tool for the production of speech. Therefore, I have come to the conclusion that having just the basic requirement to carry out a task does not necessarily equip or qualify a person to perform that task. You need more than the basic requirements.

"De man weh filt a roadside noh memba noting bout i'; di one weh step in deh neva figet."

The man who defecates by the side of the road soon forgets all about it; the one who comes along and steps in it never forgets.

Those of us who have 'stepped' into the messes created by others can identify with this saying. The persons who created the mess, having relieved themselves of their problem, move jauntily along, never giving a passing thought as to who will wallow in it. Those who step into it are left with the job of cleaning it up, and cleaning themselves off as well. How often we see this taking place on the job!

"Wass woulda learn fe mek honey, but 'im did too quick."

The wasp would have learned to make honey, but it was too quick (hasty and impetuous).

Like the bee, the wasp could have learned to make honey, but making honey requires time and patience. The wasp could not be patient enough to learn; it was more concerned with moving quickly. All that it ended up learning to do was how to make the honeycomb. At least that was the gospel, according to my grandmother. It was her elaborate way of telling me not to get ahead of myself, to slow down and be patient.

"If yuh fraid fe eye yuh cyaan' eat head."

If you are afraid of the eyes then you won't be able to eat the head, because the eyes are a part of the head.

If you are reading this and you are not familiar with the Jamaican culture, you might be wondering what this is all about. But eating parts of the head of pigs, goats, and cows is a part of the Jamaican tradition. Also, the fifth quarter (the head and feet of the animal) used to be less expensive than the flesh, and families that had many children found this to be an inexpensive way to provide meat for their families. So, our parents said all of this to say what?

Don't be a coward. You won't achieve anything by being fearful. You must be willing to confront your fears if you want to maximize your opportunities and succeed in life. Also, to be afraid of the eye when the animal is dead is also pretty silly. Therefore, I believe this is also saying that many of the things we are afraid of do not even have the power to hurt us.

"Wen yuh go a jackass yard, yuh noh fe chat bout big ears."

When you go to the donkey's yard (home) you should not talk about 'big ears'.

The donkey has big ears and will think you are criticizing him. This was just a dramatic way of telling us to be tactful.

"Wen jackass back strang dem ovaload 'im hampa."

When the donkey's back is strong, his hampers get overloaded.

Because the donkey is strong he gets more than the regular load to carry. That seems very unfair. You would think that his master would give him a special treat for being strong and carrying more than the regular load, but that is not the case. Many of us can identify with this practice at the workplace. The payment for good work is usually more work.

"Silent river run deep."

It is very quiet where the river is deep.

The water makes no sound. The rapids, on the other hand, are very noisy; one can hear the water babbling over the stones, and this is usually where the water is shallowest. This saying is used to refer to people. It is often thought that those with wisdom and knowledge and who are great thinkers are more reserved and less likely to talk their heads off than their "shallow" counterparts. It is also difficult to know what these people are capable of, because they give nothing away.

"Tun yuh han', mek fashin."

Turn your hands and make fashion (create a new fashion).

This advice was usually given during times of austerity, and could relate to almost any situation. If the usual materials to carry out a task were not available or obtainable, then the advice was to use what was available to start a new trend or create a new "fashion."

"It neva too late for a shower o' rain."

It is never too late for a shower of rain to fall.

Here, rain is used to denote misfortune. It is never too late for misfortune to overtake anyone. As long as you're alive, regardless of your past or present circumstances, the possibility exists.

"If yuh nuh mash ants yuh nuh fine 'im gut."

If you don't step on the ant, you won't find out that it has guts.

Just by looking at the ant, one might conclude that it has nothing on the inside. It is very difficult to imagine that a tiny creature like an ant would have a belly. It might therefore come as a great surprise to step on the ant and find that it really does have guts.

This saying, of course, has nothing to do with ants. Rather, it refers to those people who others tend to underestimate, to believe are quite harmless and unable to defend themselves. These quiet, unassuming people often surprise their aggressors by fighting back and refusing to be intimidated.

"Yuh neva know de luck of a lousy cyalf."

You never know the luck of a lousy calf.

You can never tell how lucky that wishy-washy calf might become. It might just surprise you. It may thrive better than all the robust-looking ones that seemed destined to prosper. The lesson to be learned is: Don't give up on anyone. A person's present circumstances are not necessarily an indicator of his or her future.

"Dawg wid too much masta sleep widout suppa."

A dog with too many masters (owners) often goes to bed without supper.

Now, how could that be? Well, as my grandmother patiently explained, if the dog had been faithful to only one owner, then that owner would have considered it his responsibility to feed the dog every day because, after all, the dog would have no other source for its food. But, knowing that the dog is serving several of them, each owner is thinking that one of the others will feed the dog, and so none of them considers it his special duty to see that the dog is fed.

What is the lesson to be learned here? Faithfulness is an important virtue. It is often said that there is safety in numbers; but, as the dog without supper could tell, that does not always work.

"De olda de moon, de brighta it shine."

The older the moon, the brighter it shines.

As the moon progresses from crescent to full over succeeding nights, it shines brighter and brighter. This might be a very difficult concept for city folk to grasp who have very little experience with moonlight; but for those of us born and raised in the country, we understand that a new crescent moon gives off very little light. However, as it moves through each phase, approaching full, its light grows ever-brighter. This is an analogy to growing old. Contrary to popular belief, as people grow older, they become more adept at many things.

"If yuh folla weh hog eat, yuh nuh eat 'im meat."

If you take the hog's diet into account, then you won't eat its meat (pork).

The young reader might have some difficulty understanding this proverb, as the diet of pigs is now far different from what it used to be years ago. Nowadays, pigs and other animals eat packaged, store-bought grain; but before the advent of the grain diet, their diet consisted of all kinds of slops and leftovers. Often, some pigs were allowed to roam around free, and these animals ate **whatever** they could find as they rummaged around. Some of the things they ate do not bear repeating.

Yet, in spite of their diet, when these animals were slaughtered, their flesh was sought after as food. No one allowed the pigs' diet to deter them from enjoying the meat of the pig.

What was the point that our parents were trying to get across to us? One should not focus on every minute detail of a circumstance or another person's behavior. To do so might cause one to overlook the attributes of that person or even miss out on great opportunities. Sometimes it is necessary to focus on the bigger picture.

"Before dawg go to bed widout suppa, im nyam cockroach."

Instead of going to bed without supper, the dog will eat cockroaches.

Insects are not usually part of a dog's diet, but the dog is not going to stand on ceremony when times are hard. It makes do with whatever is available. If cockroaches are all that's available, then the dog will eat cockroaches.

Human beings can learn a lesson from the dog. Don't go around moaning and complaining about things you wish you had. Use the resources that are available to you even if they are not what you would prefer to have.

"Yuh cyaan was'e powda pon black bud."

You cannot waste powder on a blackbird.

The literal meaning of this saying is very obvious: A blackbird has black feathers, and trying to powder it in order to change its color is a waste of time and powder. The only thing it knows how to be is a blackbird. You can put a whole lot of powder on it, and it may appear for a moment to be different; but as soon as it moves or shakes itself, the powder will fall off, and it will be just as black as it was before. Our parents were certainly not trying to teach us about blackbirds when they said this to us. What, then, did they really mean? You cannot change people, especially not from the outside. They will always revert to who they are by nature. Superficial changes do not last.

"Long run, shawt ketch."

Long run, short catch.

It is possible to be on the run for a very long time, and then be caught in a split second. I guess many fugitives can attest to that, but I do not believe that our parents were referring to fugitives when they said this. What they meant was that it is quite possible to do wrong and get away with it for a long time — only to then be caught in that same wrongdoing in a split second, when the wrongdoer least expects it.

"De wiles' bud get de neares' shot."

The wildest bird gets the nearest shot (gets shot at closest range).

One of the qualities of wild creatures is their ability to evade capture. Yet, it is amazing how close the hunter is able to get to these creatures sometimes, and how easily they can be caught. After all, it is very tedious to always be on the run and always hiding. So, although the "wild bird" has been avoiding capture for a long time, in that split second when it lets its guard down, it is captured.

This proverb is very similar in meaning to the previous one, except that it does not only speak to wrongdoers who might be on the run. It speaks as well to those who have been trying to keep out of trouble for a long time. It is a reminder that all the "bad things" you have been trying to avoid for a very long time can overtake you in a moment if you let your guard down.

"Spit in de sky, it fall in yuh face."

If you attempt to spit in the sky, the spit will fall in your face.

From a literal standpoint, this proverb is self-explanatory. Because whatever goes up must come down, the spit that you send up must come down. Also, in order to "spit in the sky" you must turn your face toward the sky. Your face will therefore be in the perfect position to receive what you sent up. The analogy to real-life situations is that whatever you do will come back to you. You will reap the consequences of your actions.

"Wha' sweet nanny goat a go run 'im belly."

What sweet nanny goat is going to run its belly (give it diarrhea).

The food that the nanny goat finds very enticing is going to give it diarrhea. Very simply put, many of the things that entice us and that we crave after are not very good for us. They often cause us harm.

"Goat always jump de weakess fence."

A goat always jumps over the weakest part of the fence.

This is very smart of the goat. It knows that it does not need to scale the fence at that particular point; just bumping against it will cause the fence to break and the goat will be able to get in anyway. Human beings seem to have learned that lesson very well from the goat. In order to get our way, we tend to attack those who are least able to stand against us.

"Have i' have i' noh want i', an' want i' want i' cyaan' get i'."

Those who have privileges and opportunities take them for granted, while there are others who crave those very things and are unable to achieve them.

Another interpretation of this proverb is that people usually crave what they don't have, but once they achieve what they craved, it loses its appeal and they treat it with scant regard.

"Dance a yard before yuh dance abrawd."

Learn to dance at home before you decide to exhibit your dancing skills abroad.

Make sure that you have practiced and perfected the skills required to do a job before you decide to display those skills in public.

"Wen fowl a trouble mangoose yuh nah hear, but wen mangoose a trouble fowl yuh hear."

When the fowl (hen) is interfering with the mongoose, no one hears, but when the mongoose is bothering the hen, everyone hears.

It is common knowledge that in altercations between the mongoose and hens or chickens, the mongoose is always the aggressor and the chickens always the victims. The chickens usually make such loud squawking noises that everyone hears them and are ready to run to their rescue. While a chicken would never taunt a mongoose, as the proverb suggests, the point to be noted here is that sometimes the victim acts as the aggressor and depends on its 'victim status' and the bad reputation of the other party to get it off the hook.

"Cuss jancro peel head, guinea hen bex."

If you criticize the crow and talk about its bald head, the guinea hen will be upset.

The reason is simple: The guinea hen is quite bald as well. Human behavior bears a great resemblance to that of the guinea hen. We take offense when we hear others criticizing our shortcomings, even when the criticism is not directed at us.

"Every jancro tink 'im pickney wite."

Every crow thinks that its offspring is white.

There is more to this proverb than meets the eye. The crow is a very black bird, and not even the crow would deny that. Why, then, would it consider its offspring to be white? This saying originated at a time in our history when no one wanted to be 'black.' Black was associated with inferiority and backwardness, while to be white was to be superior. So although the crow accepted these limitations for itself, it did not accept them for its offspring. This particular proverb speaks about the aspirations that parents have for their children. They see in their children the fulfillment of ambitions that they hoped to attain but were not able to achieve.

"Yuh haffe pay dear fi high company."

You have to pay dearly to keep high company.

Courting 'high' company will cost you dearly, because you have to strain to keep up with them. Here, high company could refer to those who are more affluent than you are or those who believe themselves to be in some way superior to you. In the case of those who have more than you do, you will probably have to spend more than you can afford in order to be like them. You might have to sacrifice your pride or your convictions to keep company with those who believe that they are in some way superior to you. At any rate, it is going to cost you dearly to court these people's friendship.

"Dawg seh him bad, but him bredanlaw beat."

The dog says his situation is bad, but that of his brother-in-law is worse.

No matter how bad the situation is that you are facing, there are always others whose circumstances are worse.

"Every tub haffe siddung pon dem own bottom."

Every tub has to sit on its own bottom.

Everyone needs to rely on himself to survive.

"Young bud noh know hurricane."

Young birds do not know hurricanes.

That is because they have never experienced one. The older birds that have been migrating every year and have seen all kinds of weather know the dangers of a hurricane. Young people, in contrast, do not have the wisdom that only experience teaches.

"Deaf ea's gi liard trouble."

The deaf person causes the liar trouble.

The liar's stories are further distorted when they are repeated by someone who does not hear very well.

"Good fu-fu neva meet good brawt."

Good fu-fu never meets some good broth (soup).

This proverb goes way back into the culture. I have never really seen fu-fu, but had it described to me when I asked my grandmother what it was. Fu-fu was yam or some other starchy tuber that was cooked, then pounded in a mortar. After that, it was shaped into balls and added to soup. According to this proverb, good fu-fu was never added to soup that was equally good. The message is that a good person never finds an equally good partner.

"Wen yuh trow stone in a hog pen, any one weh bawl out, a him get lick."

When you throw stones into a pigpen, the pig that squeals is the one that got hit.

If someone makes a general remark that angers or offends you, then the remark probably applies to you.

"Who di cap fit, mek dem wear it."

Who the cap fits, let him wear it.

This is just another way of saying the same thing expressed in the previous proverb.

"Jackass a gallop 'im noh know wah 'im back foot a seh."

The donkey is galloping (so fast) it has no idea what its hind legs are saying.

It is racing ahead so quickly it has no time to see if its hind legs are in accord with its front legs. It is not looking behind. As a matter of fact, the donkey doesn't even seem to care. To make an analogy between donkeys and human behavior is not very flattering, but without a doubt some similarities exist. Sometimes, we are so bent on what we want to do, and are so hasty in pursuing it, that we don't stop to think of possible repercussions to those close to us or even to ourselves. We just race ahead, regardless.

"If yuh noh got corn in a yuh pan, fowl naw folla yuh."

If you don't have corn in your pan, chickens won't follow after you.

Corn in the pan means food for the chickens, so the chickens will follow you around because you have something they want. If there were no corn in the pan, the chickens would most likely find another activity to pursue. Just like the chickens, people don't usually seek your company unless you have something to offer them.

"Puss sey 'im no got head fi carry coffin, so 'im naw go a dead yard."

The cat says he has no head on which to carry a coffin, so he will not go to the home of the dead.

I am sure that this proverb will make absolutely no sense to the young reader, so let me hasten to provide some background information. This saying speaks of a time in our history when funerals were not the big business that they are today. Usually, when someone died at home of natural causes — usually old age — the body remained at home until the funeral. It was washed and dressed by friends or relatives of the deceased. The coffin was made on site (at the "dead yard") by a local carpenter. When it was time for the burial, the coffin with the body was transported to the family plot by friends and family members. Sometimes the coffin was carried on their heads — hence the cat's concern. The cat is aware that it has a small head and would not be able to help in this task, so it does not go to the home of the dead person, where it might be asked to participate in this activity. I often wonder why our ancestors did not simply say to us, "If you know that you do not possess the qualifications to carry out a job, take yourself out of the running." But, of course, that was not their way; and I have to admit that this proverb presents a much more graphic and memorable picture of what they were trying to impart to us.

"Jancro seh wen im a feed im pickney pon filt, 'im nuh like hear kaka story."

When the crow has only filth with which to feed its children, it is not interested in listening to anyone or any stories deriding its means of survival.

In order to appreciate the meaning of this proverb, it is important to understand that in the Jamaican dialect, 'filt' and 'kaka' are one and the same thing. So you can understand the crow's position that in having only filth with which to feed its children, it is not interested in listening to anyone or any stories deriding its means of survival. I am sure we can all see the human connection to this proverb.

"Lucky bawn betta dan well bred."

Being born lucky is better than being from a "well-bred" family.

A person who is lucky oftentimes fares better in life than one who has all the grace and advantages of good breeding.

Carmen Earlington

Part III

Humor
(Time Fi Laugh)

Carmen Earlington

TIME FI LAUGH

Jamaicans have a great sense of humor. They are always laughing. They poke fun at everything and everyone — their politicians, clergy, neighbors, friends, and even themselves. But this laughter is not malicious; it is just lighthearted fun. Here is a look at some of their humor.

A conversation between a deaf vendor and a prospective customer at the market: (This is a very old one as you can tell by the currency mentioned.)

Customer: "Mawnin' Miss Lize."
Miss Lize: "A fowl mi a sell."
Customer: "How yuh doin' today?"
Miss Lize: "A t'ree shillin' a poun'."
Customer: "How de family?"

Miss Lize: "A don' care a damn if yuh don' want to buy; odders will."

* * * * *

A conversation between two deaf friends; they are hollering to each other across two hills.

1st Friend: "Hoy deh! A fishin' yuh a go fishin?"
2nd Friend: "No. A fishin mi a go fishin."
1st Friend: "A oh! Mi tink a fishin' yuh a go fishin'."

* * * * *

Three friends decide to weigh themselves on an electronic scale — the type that verbally states your weight.

The first friend steps up onto the scale. The scale says, "150 pounds, 150 pounds… next."

The first friend steps down and the second one steps up. The scale says, "190 pounds, 190 pounds…. next."

The second friend steps down and the third one steps up. After a split second the scale starts to beep wildly and says, "One at a time, one at a time, one at a time."

* * * * *

A politician who was reputed to be semi-illiterate was speaking to a friend about a trip he would soon be taking.

Politician: "Mi a go a San Jo-an nex' week."
Friend: "San Jo-an? Yuh mean San Juan (Wan); the "J" is silent."
Politician: "Oh."
Friend: "So when yuh a come back?"
Politician: "Mi noh sure. 'Bout Oon or Ooly soh. (Got it?)"

* * * * *

A blind man beat a man to death. He went to court. The judge asked him why he beat the man to death. The blind man said: "Mi beat him because him seh, 'lick mi an' yuh wi see', but all now mi noh see nutten."

* * * * *

A man went into a grocery store, and picked up a bottle of juice and a bag of sugar. He paid only for the juice and walked out. He was arrested for stealing the sugar. He went to court and the judge asked him why he stole the sugar. The man replied: "Yuh honor, mi noh tief no sugar. Mi look pon di back a di juice bag an it seh 'sugar free'."

* * * * *

There was a national poetry contest, and it was now down to two contestants — a Yale graduate and a Rastafarian. Both were asked to compose a poem in which the word 'Timbuktu' would be used. The Yale graduate got up and recited in grand style:

Slowly across the desert sand
Trekked a lonely caravan
Men on camels, two by two;

Yeah Mon!

Their destination – Timbuktu.

Now came the Rastafarian's turn. He strutted to the podium and said:

Me an' Tim went down de road
T'ree tief stop wi, an' want wi load
Dey were t'ree an' we were two
Soh I buck one an' Tim buck two.

Guess who won the contest.

* * * * *

A man was walking along the road when he came upon two men arguing about how stupid their sons were. He paused to listen.

1st Man:	"I have a bwoy, 'im fool yuh si."
2nd Man:	"No matta how 'im fool 'im cyaan' fool like my son."
1st Man:	"A'right, watch dis. Junior?"
Boy:	"Yes, daddy!"
1st Man:	"Come 'ere."

The boy comes running. He hands the boy a $20.00 bill and says,

"I want yu to tek dis $20.00 an' buy mi a cyar."

The boy takes the money and runs off down the road.

The second man says,

"Well, mek mi show yuh seh my son more fool."

2nd Man: "Calvin?"
2nd boy: "Yes, sah." The boy comes running.
2nd Man: "Mi want yuh fi go to de bar dung de road and look if yuh see mi dere. If yuh see mi tell mi to come 'ere right aweh."
2nd boy: "Yes sah." The boy took off at great speed down the road.

The listener could hardly believe his ears. He shook his head and continued on his journey down the road. After a few minutes he came upon the two boys having a heated conversation. The first boy was saying, "Yuh know my fahda really stupid. 'Im gimme dis $20.00 fi buy 'im a cyar an' 'im doan' even tell mi what kine a cyar mi fi buy — wedda 'im want a Honda or a Toyota or what."

Hear the second boy.

"My fahda more stupid dan your fahda. 'Im sen' mi dung 'ere fi look if mi see 'im, but 'im have a cell phone; 'im coulda call."

* * * * *

A man went to the doctor with his two ears burned.

The doctor asked, "Why are your ears so badly burnt?"

His reply was, "Bwoy docta, mi did a ion mi clothes an' ting fi go a wuk an' tru because mi a hurry mi pick up di ion an' ansa it instead a di cell fone..."

The doctor's reply was, "But, Boss, I can understand why one ear would've been burnt, but why is it that both ears are burnt?"

The man replied, "Nuh di dyam FOOL call mi back doc!"

GLOSSARY

A

Ackee	national fruit
Anansi, anancy	spider (folk hero, lauded for his cunning ability to outwit others)

B

bex	vex
bonnet	hood (of a car)
brawt	broth
bredda	brother
bway, bwoy	boy
bruk	break
buck	butt (with the head)

C

chaka-chaka	untidy

chattabox	extremely talkative person; a motor-mouth
chaw	chew
coolie	someone of East Indian descent
craben	greedy
craw	stomach (of a bird)
cuss-cuss	cursing, bad-mouthing
cyaan'	cannot

D

dawg	dog
degeh	only (one degeh one)
deh, dere	there
dundus	albino
duppy	ghost
dutty	(1) dirty, (2) ground

E

Extra	show off, pretending to be what you are not

F

fa'as	interfering, not minding your own business
fe, fi	for
fool-fool	stupid
foot	refers to any part of the leg

G

gal	girl
gimme	give me
grudgeful	envious
grung	ground
gwine	going to

H

haffe	have to
heng	hang
hush	sorry (often said when you step on someone's toe accidentally)

I

Indicator	signal light (on a motor vehicle)

J
jancro	crow
jinnal	trickster
Juk, jook	poke or pierce

K
ketch	catch
kin teet	grin (a phony smile)
kuya	look here
ku pon dis	look at this

L
lef	leave
leggo	let go
liad	liar
lick	hit
licky-licky	greedy, liking freebies

M
macka	thorn
magitch	maggots
mash	break, smash

mashmout	lost many teeth (needing dentures)
mawnin'	morning
mean	stingy, tight-fisted
mek	let (mek mi tell yuh how it go) make (mek one fi mi)
modda	mother
mumma	mother (derogatory)

N

naw	not
noh	not (a noh dat one; it's not that one) don't (noh go deh; don't go there)
nuff	a lot of
nutten	nothing
nyam	eat
nyam an' go weh	eat and leave (without assisting in the preparation or cleaning up)

O

Ongle	only

P

pastcha	pasture
patoo	owl
pickney	child, children
puss	cat

Q

quatty	one and a half pennies (old Jamaican currency)

R

red (y)eye	covetous (wanting what others have)
rubber	eraser
romp	play

S

salt	unlucky
sinting	something
skin	peel (when referring to fruits or vegetables)
sleeping policeman	speed bump

swipple — slippery

T
tan — stay
tidde — today
twang — accent (putting on a false accent)
tumble dung — fall down

U
Unoo — you (pl.)

W
walkbout — not staying in one place travel a lot
wass — wasp
weh — where or what
windscreen — windshield

Y
Ya(h) — here
Yuh — you (sing.)

CPSIA information can be obtained
at www.ICGtesting.com
Printed in the USA
LVOW04s1054091216
516560LV00010B/112/P

9 781634 984102